BRAZILIAN PORTUGUESE CHILDREN'S BOOK

Robinson Crusoe
(English and Brazilian Portuguese Edition)

TIMOTHY DYSON

©Copyright, 2016, by Timothy Dyson and Maestro Publishing Group
All rights reserved.

No part of this book may be reproduced or transmitted in any form or by any means, electronic or mechanical, including photocopying, recording or by any information storage and retrieval system, without permission in writing of the copyright owner.

Printed in the United States of America.

ABOUT THE BOOK

Raise your children in a bilingual fashion with this dual language coloring book. Let your child travel through the exciting journey of Robinson Crusoe while learning both English and another language at the same time. This coloring book is a must for those wanting to raise their children in a bilingual fashion.

CONTENTS

Plate 1 3

Plate 2 5

Plate 3 7

Plate 4 9

Plate 5 11

Plate 6 13

Plate 7 15

Plate 8 17

This page intentionally left blank.

Ever since Robinson Crusoe was a boy, he dreamed of a life of adventure on the high seas.

Desde quando Robinson Crusoe era um menino, ele sonhava com uma vida de aventuras em alto mar.

Plate 1

Forty miles off the coast of South America, Crusoe's ship was sunk by a wild storm and he was the sole survivor.

Quarenta milhas da costa da América do Sul, o navio de Crusoé foi afundado por uma forte tempestade e ele foi o único sobrevivente.

Plate 2

He made his way to land, which he came to know as The Island of Despair.

Ele encontrou seu caminho para a terra, que ele veio a conhecer como a Ilha de Desespero.

Plate 3

He saved some tools and other items from the shipwreck and set himself to making the island his new home.

Ele salvou algumas ferramentas e outros itens do naufrágio e começou a fazer da ilha sua nova casa.

Plate 4

After discovering natives on the island, Crusoe freed one of their captives, brought him back to his dwelling, named him Friday and taught him English.

Depois de descobrir os nativos da ilha, Crusoé libertou um dos seus cativos, trouxe de volta para a sua casa, o chamou de Sexta-feira e lhe ensinou Inglês.

Plate 5

Crusoe and Friday discovered more captives, helped to free them and sent them to the mainland to bring back men who can help build a ship.

Crusoé e Sexta-feira descobriram mais cativos, ajudaram a libertá-los e os mandaram para o continente para trazer de volta homens que pudessem ajudar a construir um navio.

Plate 6

But fate intervened; an English ship arrived before the other men returned, and Crusoe struck a bargain with its captain that would return him and Friday to England.

Mas o destino interveio; um navio Inglês chegou antes dos outros homens, Crusoé e o capitão chegaram a um acordo que iria levar ele e Sexta-feira de volta a Inglaterra.

Plate 7

With nothing to return to in England, Crusoe and Friday made their way to Portugal, encountering hungry wolves amid the mountain pass, the last in Crusoe's series of grand adventures.

Crusoé e Sexta-feira não tinham nada para levar para a Inglaterra e fizeram o seu caminho para Portugal, onde encontraram lobos famintos no meio da passagem pela montanha, a última de uma série de grandes aventuras de Crusoé.

Plate 8

This page intentionally left blank.

ABOUT THE BOOK

Raise your children in a bilingual fashion with this dual language coloring book. Let your child travel through the exciting journey of Robinson Crusoe while learning both English and another language at the same time. This coloring book is a must for those wanting to raise their children in a bilingual fashion.

CPSIA information can be obtained
at www.ICGtesting.com
Printed in the USA
BVHW01s1839160418
513526BV00008B/252/P